What the fence sees

BETH PHILLIPS

To order additional copies of this book, contact:
Xlibris
844-714-8691
www.Xlibris.com
Orders@Xlibris.com

ISBN: Softcover   978-1-6698-0278-5
         EBook   978-1-6698-0279-2

Print information available on the last page

Rev. date: 12/07/2021

In the late 1940's their were two girls in the same class in high school who had no idea they were destined to become sister-in-laws.

One of the girls sang with her sisters on a nearby radio station and worked in a shoe factory and the other girl helped her father with their family farm.

Gerrie and Virginia did not have a close relationship in high school but were later acquainted when Gerrie was introduced to Virginia's brother Harold.

Virginia and Harold were sister and brother respectively. With Harold being older and having been born in 1930.

Both girls attended a high school in New England as well as Harold. A common interest in a particular discipline united the two.

After an appropriate courtship the two married. After being unable to have children of their own they decided to adopt .

Middle 1960's they adopted two children. These two girls went on to attend the local elementary school.

Many times the usual childhood behaviors resulted in trips to the school principal. Summers were fun with lots of fun activities including water skiing, wave surfing, picnics and camping .

Due to a job opportunity in one of the southern US states the family moved in the middle to late 1970's.

Vacations became modified in the southern states with shell hunting on beaches and becoming acclimated to a new weather patterns which included a consistent rain each day in the summers.

The two girls finished high school and some college and then went on to start their own families.

One became a teacher and married a doctor in the early months of the year 2001.

Teaching in itself proved to be quite a challenge when in 2001 with an over confident sense of stability, Beth found out she was at the last minute a unit loss which meant a trip to the teaching pool.

The trip to the teaching pool resulted in a new opportunity at a brand néw school.

That néw school proved to be both rewarding and learning experiences of many varieties. Those included the inception of the "Teacher Review." The Teacher review is not in a peanut butter and Jelly sandwich format. In terms of I like the way you do this but improvement is needed here.

The next teaching job was a private school which was not covered under the local state retirement plan.

A wonderful opportunity none the less. Lifelong friendships were formed.

Harold and Gerrie with the house to themselves decided to join the RV family. They took many trips to the northern southeastern United States and by working for the Army core of Engineers that allowed them to stay longer.

Shortly after marriage Beth became involved in helping out at the local animal shelter.

Beth adopted two dogs and later two more.

Life continued with usual annual check- ups at the nearby vet clinic . Later a man would have a unique impact as a veterinarian himself and also a member of an organization that took pets to visit the elderly and infirmed.

Another teaching opportunity presented itself and this time started out as a subbing job which turned into a full time job.

This job lasted two years with a requirement to pass a competency test in the subject of tractor mechanics. Unable to reach this goal, that job ended.

But nothing happens by mistake and a new career blossomed.

Life continued with the usual of having dogs including baths and trips to dog parks. As well as the usual challenges associated with living in a hurricaine riddled area of the US.

Life in the years of 2010-2020 saw many generations neighborhood cats that had kittens and the neighbors that took them in . Household pet fish that had fish and those fish that had fish . Harold and Gerrie continued their RV life until a fall forced them to sell and retire from RV life.

Lynne married and had a son who later had a daughter of his own. The normal mile stone birthdays were fun and filled with cruises and backyard cook-outs. Life appeared to be fun filled but what the fence saw was something different.

In August of 2014 Beth opened a small home dog grooming business and in November of that year Harold came down with a mysterious illness that manifested itself by him tugging at the curtains in his house and later which ended with an ambulance being called and a trip to the hospital that he would not return .

The opening of the dog grooming business required many documents including permits and tax related items such as Business EIN numbers, LLC, insurance, etc. The business proved to be not a liveable source of income and unrealistic unless one had a second job . Although even though adding pet sitting services and home health aids services it did not add up to a combination of jobs one could live on .

Another teaching opportunity presented itself in terms of a subbing job.

The opening of the business moved forward. Equipment was ordered . Air conditioning was installed in the garage dog business by the next door neighbor .

A security system was installed by a local citizen.

A clientele was built up through many advertising tactics. Including newspaper flyer ads, business cards in the local vet offices. Ads in newspapers proved beneficial and the new housekeeper became a character . A lady who was picky and complained quite frequently as a dog grooming client.

The friendly next door neighbor who always offered a hand with gardening.

In early December of 2014 Harold had developed a brain bleed . The procedure required the signature of Gerrie in which she declined. Who influenced her ? The houseguest? The doctor? The younger sister?

A simple procedure . Yet it was denied . Turned down by Gerrie.

Shortly after Harold went to a hospice facility .

A day or to before the middle of December after 5pm Harold transitioned to the next life .

Shortly after the family home was put up for sale.

About that time other strange activities ensued. Gerrie put the house on the market planning a move to New Jersey. Houseguest was hospitalized a few months later .

Harold had asked Beth daughter to agree to a scheme in which she was to say she lost her key in an effort to get the key back from the houseguest. Houseguest had been a former neighbor . Who when facing hard times often borrowed water and electricity from neighbors . One wonders why Harold did not want houseguest to have a key . Also why he wouldn't just say "I don't want to hurt your feelings, but I don't feel comfortable with your having a key." Shortly after the passing of Harold in the late days of December, Gerrie moved to New Jersey to live with Lynne.

The houseguest was hospitalized.

Beth continued with dog business.

In the middle years of 2010, Beth attended a long awaited reunion with her biological family. When returning to Florida and finding out her two best helpers were leaving and moving to New York and several of the dog clients slowly transitioning to the next life an opportunity for writing. Another opportunity presented itself to train in network security.

Beth adopted a puppy of Australian Shepard descent and the handsome Air Force office started screaming "I don't want another dog ." Resulting in the dog being rehomed determined to maintain peace Beth bought a small mobile home nearby but elected to stay in the ranch house for the benefit of the pets . In the late months of the 2020 an opportunity presented itself for Beth to play the star spangled banner at a nearby auction.

As she diligently practiced little did she know of the events to follow. While sitting at a traffic light her car was hit from a behind from a car going full speed. Again relying on the friends she thought she had the totalled car was replaced by a small check from the insurance company. Friends helped. Brought writing supplies. It was at this time she decided to adopt two baby hamsters. Very loving and hating to see them separated - took them in. Quite amount of research went into creating the healthiest habitats possible for them. Replacing plastic houses with wooden ones. Replacing the 10 gallon fish tank with a 20 gallon fish tank. Replacing the paper bedding with a more appropriate bedding . Next came the alternate play habitat. Top soil .

Fourth of July came and went with all pets enjoying the holiday sparklers.

At this time Brownie the street cat appeared.

Beth Phillips' upcoming book talks about stories and notes from the Grooming table.

Printed in the United States
by Baker & Taylor Publisher Services